WHSmith

Revise
English

KS2: YEAR 3

Age 7–8

Louis Fidge

First published 2007
exclusively for WHSmith by
Hodder Murray, a member of the Hodder Headline group
338 Euston Road
London
NW1 3BH

Impression number 10 9 8 7 6 5 4 3 2 1
Year 2008 2007

A CIP record for this book is available from the British Library.

Cover illustration by Sally Newton Illustrations

Typeset by Fakenham Photosetting Limited, Fakenham, Norfolk

ISBN – 13 978 0 34094270 3

Printed and bound in Italy.

Contents

The *WHS Revise* series

The *WHS Revise* books enable you to help your child revise and practise important skills taught in school. These skills form part of the National Curriculum and will help your child to improve his or her Maths and English.

Testing in schools

During their time at school all children will undergo a variety of tests. Regular testing is a feature of all schools. It is carried out:

- *informally* – in everyday classroom activities your child's teacher is continually assessing and observing your child's performance in a general way
- *formally* – more regular formal testing helps the teacher check your child's progress in specific areas.

Testing is important because:

- it provides evidence of your child's achievement and progress
- it helps the teacher decide which skills to focus on with your child
- it helps compare how different children are progressing.

The importance of revision

Regular revision is important to ensure your child remembers and practises skills he or she has been taught. These books will help your child revise and test his or her knowledge of some of the things he or she will be expected to know. They will help you prepare your child to be in a better position to face tests in school with confidence.

How to use this book

Units

This book is divided into forty units, each focusing on one key skill. Each unit begins with a **Remember** section, which introduces and revises essential information about the particular skill covered. If possible, read and discuss this with your child to ensure he or she understands it.

This is followed by a **Have a go** section, which contains a number of activities to help your child revise the topic thoroughly and use the skill effectively. Usually, your child should be able to do these activities fairly independently.

Revision tests

There are four revision tests in this book (pages 46–53). These test the skills covered in the preceding units and assess your child's progress and understanding. They can be marked by you or by your child. Your child should fill in his or her test score for each test in the space provided. This will provide a visual record of your child's progress and an instant sense of confidence and achievement.

Parents' notes

The parents' notes (on pages 54–55) provide you with brief information on each skill and explain why it is important.

Answers

Answers to the unit questions and tests may be found on pages 56–64.

Unit 1: Full stops and capital letters

Remember

A sentence must **begin** with a **capital letter**.
Many sentences **end** with a **full stop**.

My bike is red and yellow.

Have a go

1. Write these sentences correctly.

   a the sun is shining

   b the sky is blue

   c there are some clouds

   d it is very hot

   e we are going to the park

   f in the park there is a lake

2. Here are some sentences that have run together.
   Write them again as pairs of proper sentences.

   a the driver stopped the bus the boy got off

   b the woman came home from the shop she had some apples in her bag

   c the firefighters stopped at the fire they soon put it out

   d the boy liked his baby sister sometimes she smiled at him

   e the bird built a nest it laid several eggs in it

Unit 2: Word-building with phonemes

Remember

A **phoneme** is the **smallest unit of sound** in a word.
A phoneme may be made up of **one or more letters** which make **one sound**.

g + oa + t = goat

(3 phonemes)

Have a go

1 Do the phoneme sums. Write the words. Read the words you make.

a sh + ee + p = sheep

b b + oa + t = boat

c ch + ar + t = chart

d d + r + ea + m = dream

e p + l + ay = play

f r + oa + d = road

g t + oy = toy

h g + r + ow = grow

i l + ou + d = loud

j j + oi + n = join

2 Choose the correct phoneme to complete each word.

a	b	c	d	e
oo / oa	ow / oo	ir / ar	or / ur	ay / ai

f_oo_t	c_ow_	g_ir_l	p_or_se	pl_ay_

f	g	h	i	j
oi / ai	ee / ea	aw / au	ue / ie	ew / ow

n_ai_l	s_ea_t	cl_aw_	gl_ue_	sn_ow_

Unit 3: Nouns

Remember

Words that **name** things are called **nouns**.
A noun may be the name of a **person**, **place** or **thing**.

teacher

school

book

Have a go

1. Fill in the missing nouns.

hospital fence museum detective staple plumber

a A detective investigates crimes.

b A ______________ fits and repairs water pipes.

c A ______________ is where sick people are cared for.

d A ______________ is where old and interesting things are kept.

e A ______________ is used to clip two pieces of paper together.

f A ______________ is used to divide two pieces of land.

2. Name these groups of nouns.

a cabbage, potato, carrot vegetables

b tennis, cricket, swimming ______________

c drums, piano, trumpet ______________

d apple, banana, pear ______________

e pen, pencil, crayon ______________

f trousers, jacket, hat ______________

g knife, fork, spoon ______________

h car, bike, coach ______________

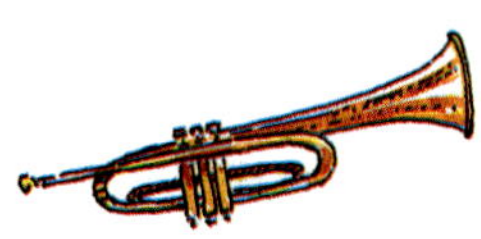

Unit 4: Commas in lists

Remember

We use commas to **separate items in a list**.
We do **not** usually put a comma before the word **and** in a list.

Out of my window I can see a bus, a lorry, two cars and a motorbike.

Have a go

1 Put in the missing commas in these sentences.

a Sunday Monday Tuesday and Wednesday are days of the week.

b For my birthday I had some paints a book a game and a jigsaw.

c A gardener needs a rake a spade a fork and some shears.

d Sarah has a thin face black hair brown eyes and a small nose.

e On holiday I visited France Germany Italy and Spain.

f In the woods I saw a fox a squirrel some birds and a hedgehog.

2 Complete these sentences in your own words.

a Four things I like to eat are ______________________________.

b The first four months of the year are ______________________________.

c In the fridge at home we keep ______________________________.

d The names of three children in my class are ______________________________.

e Some foods I like are ______________________________.

f The colours of the rainbow are ______________________________.

g Four countries in Europe are ______________________________.

Unit 5: Letter patterns – *le*

Remember

Always look carefully at words to see if you can spot any **common letter patterns**.

An app**le** and a cand**le** are near the tab**le**.

Have a go

1. Make these words. One has been done for you.

a

han, nee, mid, la, cra → dle →

handle
____
____
____
____

b

an, sin, ea, jin, jun → gle →

____
____
____
____
____

2. Sort these words into groups according to the letter patterns they end in:

sparkle grumble rifle purple tickle
table title simple feeble trifle
raffle example battle muffle ankle

ble words	fle words	kle words	ple words	tle words

Unit 6: Compound words (1)

Remember

Compound words are made up of **two smaller words joined together**.

rain + bow = rainbow

Have a go

Make these compound words.

Write them here.
Read the words you make.

hand	writing	**handwriting**
wind	mill	
bath	room	
book	case	
birth	day	
foot	step	
pan	cake	
black	bird	
sun	shine	
car	pet	
some	one	
any	way	
no	body	

Unit 7: Verbs – present tense

Remember

When something is happening **now** (in the **present**) we write the verb in the **present tense**. We can write a verb in the present tense in **two ways**.

I **leap**.

I **am leaping**.

Have a go

1. Complete each pair of sentences.

a I jump. I am jumping.
b I catch. I am ________.
c I cook. I am ________.
d I speak. I am ________.
e I walk. I am ________.
f I sing. I am ________.
g I look. I am ________.
h I draw. I am ________.

2. Write the correct form of the verb in each gap. Take care with the spelling!

a A swan is (swim) ____________ in the water.
b Some frogs are (hop) ____________ along.
c The lady is (drive) ____________ a van.
d The man is (bake) ____________ a cake.
e My dog is (wag) ____________ his tail.
f The boy is (skip) ____________.
g Sam is (smile) ____________.
h The sun is (shine) ____________.
i I am ____________ (bite) a crunchy apple.
j Tara is ____________ (clap) her hands.

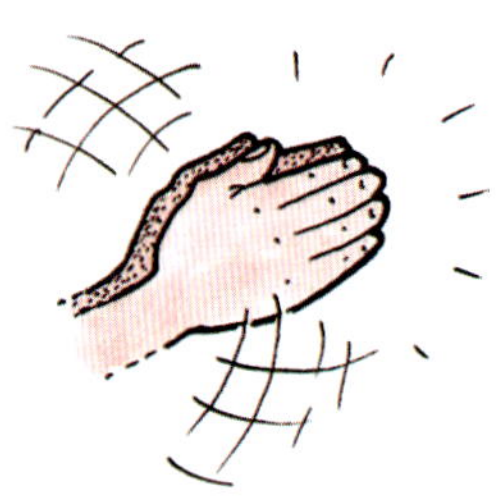

Unit 8: Alphabetical order

Remember

It is important to understand how to organise things in **alphabetical order**. Many books are arranged in alphabetical order.

alligator bear camel

These words are organised according to their **first** letter.

sheep snake squirrel

These words are organised according to their **second** letter.

Have a go

1. Write these animals in alphabetical order according to their first letters.

a bat antelope donkey cat

b panda mouse leopard tiger giraffe

2. Now write these names in alphabetical order according to their second letters.

a hamster horse hippo hedgehog

b cheetah camel crocodile cow

c reindeer rhino rook rabbit

d pelican puppy pony panda pig

e orangutan ox octopus owl ostrich

Unit 9: Rhyming (1)

Remember

We must **listen** carefully to identify words that **rhyme**.
We also need to **look** carefully.
Some **rhyming words** contain the **same letter patterns**.

Do you like the r**ain** in Sp**ain**?

Have a go

Match up the pairs of rhyming words.

Write them here and <u>underline</u> the common letter patterns.

found	voice	
bread	wire	
choice	round	<u>f**ound**</u> r**<u>ound</u>**
claw	ledge	
fire	tread	
dear	niece	
hedge	paw	
spice	near	
piece	marry	
carry	twice	

Unit 10: Prefixes – *un* and *dis*

Remember

A **prefix** is a **group of letters** we add on to the **front** of a word.
Prefixes change the **meaning** of the word.
Adding the prefixes **un** and **dis** makes the words mean the **opposite**.

happy

unhappy

agree

disagree

Have a go

1 Choose **un** or **dis** to complete each word.

a ____well b ____agree c ____appear d ____lucky

e ___comfortable f ___obedient g ____lock h ____appoint

i ____honest j ___pack

2 Add **un** or **dis** in each gap to give the word the opposite meaning.

a Sam <u>un</u>locked her suitcase.

b The two children always ___agreed with each other.

c I feel very ___lucky today.

d My dog is very ___obedient.

e The man was very ___honest.

f The sports car ___appeared in a flash.

g Tom looked rather ___well.

h The armchair was very ___comfortable.

i Ben ___packed the shopping in the trolley.

j I ___like sprouts very much.

Unit 11: Using adjectives (1)

Remember

An **adjective** is a **describing** word.
An adjective gives us more **information about a noun**.

a **fierce** lion

Have a go

1 Underline the adjective that describes each noun.
One has been done for you.

a a <u>crunchy</u> apple
b an exciting story
c the old lady
d a windy day
e some ripe bananas
f a tiny baby
g some buzzing bees
h an angry bull
i a beautiful hat
j some golden sand
k the blunt pencil
l a tall building

2 Choose the most suitable adjective to describe each noun.

a a ____________ noise (loud, bold)
b a ____________ weight (heavy, bright)
c a ____________ mark (quiet, dirty)
d a ____________ drink (fizzy, wide)
e an ____________ bottle (empty, excited)
f a ____________ prince (soft, handsome)
g a ____________ ruler (wobbly, straight)
h a ____________ sea (thin, rough)

Unit 12: Silent letters – *k* and *w*

Remember

Some words contain **silent letters**.
We cannot hear them when we say the words.

knee

wrist

Have a go

1. Make these words. One has been done for you.

a

k	not	knot
	now	______
	nee	______
	nife	______
	nock	______

b

w	rap	______
	reck	______
	rist	______
	rite	______
	rong	______

2. Write the word from above that rhymes with:

neck	→	wreck
life	→	
blow	→	
slap	→	
spot	→	
white	→	
shock	→	
tree	→	
list	→	
song	→	

Unit 13: Suffixes – *ful* and *less*

Remember

A **suffix** is a **group of letters** we add to the **end** of a word.
We can change some **nouns** into **adjectives** by adding the suffix **ful** or **less**.

care + ful = careful
(noun) (adjective)

care + less = careless
(noun) (adjective)

Have a go

1 Make some adjectives. Read the words you make.

a **help** → **ful** helpful; **less** helpless
b **thought** → **ful** ____; **less** ____
c **pain** → **ful** ____; **less** ____
d **colour** → **ful** ____; **less** ____
e **hope** → **ful** ____; **less** ____
f **power** → **ful** ____; **less** ____
g **use** → **ful** ____; **less** ____
h **rest** → **ful** ____; **less** ____
i **thank** → **ful** ____; **less** ____
j **harm** → **ful** ____; **less** ____

2 Take the suffix off each adjective. Write the noun you are left with. (Sometimes you may have to alter the spelling a little!)

a pitiful pity
b successful ____
c merciless ____
d speechless ____
e respectful ____
f mindless ____
g friendless ____
h wonderful ____
i beautiful ____
j senseless ____

Unit 14: Using apostrophes (1)

Remember

We can **shorten** some words by missing some letters out.
We put an **apostrophe** to show where letters are missing.

Don't do that!

Don't = Do not

Have a go

1 Match up the shorter and longer forms of these words.

I'm	they are
we've	it is
they're	I am
she's	they will
wouldn't	we have
they'll	she is
you're	was not
it's	would not
wasn't	does not
doesn't	you are

2 Write the shorter form of these:

a would not = wouldn't

b they are = ____________

c we have = ____________

d I am = ____________

e you are = ____________

f she is = ____________

g was not = ____________

h they will = ____________

i does not = ____________

Unit 15: Singular and plural (1)

Remember

Singular means **one**. **Plural** means **more than one**.
When a word ends with **s**, **sh**, **ch** or **x** we add **es** to make it plural.

one coach

lots of coaches

Have a go

Complete this chart.

singular	plural
one fox	lots of ________
one kiss	lots of ________
one ________	lots of churches
one ________	lots of dishes
one box	lots of ________
one ________	lots of glasses
one ________	lots of buses
one wish	lots of ________
one ________	lots of matches
one arch	lots of ________
one brush	lots of ________
one ________	lots of stitches

Unit 16: Personal pronouns

Remember

A **pronoun** is a word that **takes the place of a noun**. A **personal pronoun** takes the place of the **name of a person or thing**.

Tom scored a goal when **he** (Tom) kicked the ball.

Here are all the **personal pronouns**.

I	me	we	us	you	he	him	she	her	it	they	them

Have a go

1 Underline all the personal pronouns in these sentences.

a I love strawberries.

b We are going to the park.

c Can you swim?

d The girl cried when she fell over.

e The old man sat down because he was tired.

f The police caught the men and put them in jail.

g I threw a stick and the dog picked it up.

2 Choose the best pronoun to complete each sentence.

a When the girl got up, (he, she) ________ got dressed.

b Are (it, you) ________ good at maths?

c (They, It) ________ is very sunny today.

d The children laughed as (she, they) ________ ran home.

e (I, You) ________ am very hungry.

f I like Edward but (we, he) ________ does not like (us, me) ________ .

Unit 17: Subject and verb agreement (1)

Remember

Every sentence must have a **verb**.
Every verb must have a **subject** (the person or thing that goes with the verb).
The subject and verb must always **agree**.

The dog bark. ☒ The dog barks. ☑

Have a go

1 Underline the subject in each sentence.
Circle the verb in each sentence.

a Birds sing.
b A horse gallops.
c The snake hisses.
d Some children giggle.
e Emma is running.
f The baby smiled.
g A telephone rings.
h My dad snores.

2 Choose the correct form of the verb to go with each subject.

a A duck __________ . (quack, quacks)
b Most owls __________ . (hoot, hoots)
c The children __________ out. (go, goes)
d Where __________ you live? (do, does)
e Some children __________ fair hair. (has, have)
f A snail __________ slowly. (move, moves)
g Lions __________ . (roar, roars)
h A cow __________ . (moo, moos)

Unit 18: Conjunctions – *and* and *but*

Remember

A **conjunction** is a **joining** word. We use a **conjunction** to join two short sentences together to make one longer sentence.

The cat woke up. It walked away. The cat woke up **and** it walked away.

Have a go

1. Write each pair of sentences as one long sentence.
   Join them with the conjunction **and**.

   a The alien opened its mouth. It began to speak.

   ____

   b Edward called for Sam. They went to the park.

   ____

   c Lucy went to bed. She read a book.

   ____

   d The spider spun a web. It caught a fly.

   ____

   e Tom got some seeds. He planted them in the garden.

   ____

2. Now join these sentences with the conjunction **but**.

   a Kate loves chips. Emma hates them.

   ____

   b I tried the key. It would not open the door.

   ____

   c My dog loves walks. It does not like having a bath.

   ____

   d The car went fast. It made a lot of noise.

   ____

Unit 19: Words with similar meanings

Remember

Synonyms are words that have **similar meanings**.

jump **leap** **bound**

Have a go

Match up the pairs of verbs with similar meanings.

Write them here.

cry	brush	
sweep	chew	
speak	sob	**cry sob**
eat	close	
shut	race	
run	talk	
grab	groan	
moan	grasp	
open	answer	
reply	unlock	
end	bite	
chew	start	
begin	finish	

Unit 20: Using speech marks (1)

Remember

In **writing** we write the words the person actually says inside **speech marks**.

Claire said, "I like to watch TV."

Have a go

1 Fill in the missing speech marks.

a Emma said, I like skating.

b Ben said, Let's play a video game.

c Edward said, I want to go for a bike ride.

d Anna asked, What is for dinner?

e Ali asked, Where is Tom?

f Sarah said, Pass me my bag, please.

g Nicky exclaimed, What a lovely present!

h Rehannah shouted, Look at this!

2 Choose a word from the box and write what each animal said.

Squeak Hiss Neigh Baa Gobble Quack Woof Buzz

a The horse said, "____________." b The duck said, "____________."

c The snake said, "____________." d The turkey said, "____________."

e The dog said, "____________." f The bee said, "____________."

g The mouse said, "____________." h The sheep said, "____________."

Unit 21: Using question marks

Remember

A **question** always **begins** with a **capital letter** and **ends** with a **question mark**.

Have a go

1. Write these questions correctly.

   a what is your name ______________________

   b where do you live ______________________

   c how old are you ______________________

   d when is your birthday ______________________

   e which school do you go to ______________________

2. Here are the answers to some questions.
   Write what you think each question was.

Questions	Answers
a ______________________	It is ten o'clock.
b ______________________	Paris is the capital of France.
c ______________________	I would like an apple.
d ______________________	She is my teacher.
e ______________________	It is on the table.
f ______________________	Blue is my favourite colour.
g ______________________	We are going to Spain this year.
h ______________________	This present is for you.

Unit 22: Finding the missing phonemes

Remember

A **phoneme** is the **smallest unit of sound** in a word.

A phoneme may be made up of **one or more letters** which make **one sound**.

c + oa + t = coat
(3 phonemes)

Have a go

Work out the missing phoneme in each word. Read the words you make.

a  b + ir + d — bird	b  c + ___ + ch — ______	c  g + r + a + ___ — ______	d  ch + ___ — ______
e  d + r + ___ — ______	f  b + ___ + k — ______	g  m + ___ + th — ______	h  t + ___ + ch — ______
i  c + ___ + n — ______	j  c + r + ___ + n — ______	k  ch + ___ + ch — ______	l  sh + ___ + k — ______

Unit 23: Proper nouns

Remember

A **proper noun** is the **particular** name of a **person**, **place** or **thing**.
A proper noun always **begins** with a **capital letter**.

Have a go

1. Rewrite these proper nouns correctly.

a edinburgh ________________ b amy ________________

c wednesday ________________ d ford road ________________

e king henry ________________ f daily mail ________________

g rome ________________ h april ________________

i humpty dumpty ________________ j newcastle united ________________

2. Rewrite these sentences correctly.

a mrs brown is my teacher.

____

b on holiday sarah visited paris in france.

____

c last thursday jamie went to see london bridge.

____

d mrs shah was reading the daily telegraph.

____

e we are staying in the grand hotel in dover.

____

f the plane from mumbai landed at gatwick airport.

____

Unit 24: Commas in sentences

Remember

Commas are used to **separate** any **extra bits** that are **added** to the **beginning** or **ending** of sentences.

Have a go

1. Fill in the missing comma in each sentence.

a Sam come here.

b Where are you Mum?

c May I have an apple please?

d Dad look at me!

e Sorry Miss.

f What's the matter Mr Jordan?

g Sarah stop pushing me.

h I can't do it can I?

i Ben stop at once!

j I'll go to bed shall I?

2. Rewrite each sentence correctly.

a may i have a drink please

____

b no you can't

____

c tom pass me my bag

____

d yes here it is

____

e sam would you like a cake

____

f i would like a doughnut i think

____

g stop cheating jo

____

h that's not fair mum

____

Unit 25: Letter patterns – *igh*

Remember

Always look carefully at words to see if you can spot any **common letter patterns**.

a fr**igh**t in the n**igh**t

Have a go

1 Make these words. Read the words you make.

igh

h**igh**___ th_____ s_____

high___ _____ _____

ight

r**ight**___ n_____ f_____ l_____ m_____ s_____ t_____

_____ _____ _____ _____ _____ _____ _____

2 Write the words ending in **igh** in alphabetical order.

_____ _____ _____

3 Write the words ending in **ight** in alphabetical order.

_____ _____ _____ _____ _____ _____ _____

4 Fill in each gap with a word from above.

a My jeans are too _____________.

b The _____________ mountains were a lovely _____________.

c I got all my spellings _____________.

d I woke up in the middle of the _____________.

e I _____________ have to turn off the _____________.

Unit 26: Compound words (2)

Remember

Compound words are made up of **two smaller words joined together**.

snow + 
man = 
snowman

Have a go

Work out what compound words these picture sums make.

a  +  = ladybird

b  +  = ____________

c  +  = ____________

d  +  = ____________

e  +  = ____________

f  +  = ____________

g 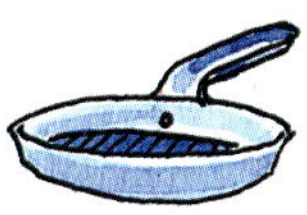 +  = ____________

h  +  = ____________

i  +  = ____________

j 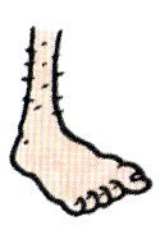 +  = ____________

Unit 27: Verbs – past tense

Remember

When we are writing about something that happened **in the past**, we use the **past tense** of verbs.

Today I **am playing** football.

Yesterday I **played** cricket.

This is happening **now**, so the verb is in the **present tense**.

This happened in the **past**, so the verb is in the **past tense**.

Have a go

1 Complete each pair of sentences in the chart.

Present tense	Past tense
Today I splash.	Yesterday I splashed .
Today I jump.	Yesterday I __________ .
Today I play.	Yesterday I __________ .
Today I walk.	Yesterday I __________ .
Today I paint.	Yesterday I __________ .
Today I help.	Yesterday I __________ .

2 Write the past tense of the verb in each gap. Take care with the spelling!

a The kangaroo (hop) __________ through the desert.

b Last week I (rip) __________ my trousers.

c Just now, a woman (smile) __________ at me.

d Before I went to bed, I (try) __________ to do my homework.

e Last night, my dad (snore) __________ in his sleep.

f I felt so sad I (sob) __________ all night.

Unit 28: Dictionary work – definitions

Remember

A **dictionary** may be used to help you find the **definition** (meaning) of a word.

mechanic A **mechanic** repairs machines and engines.

Have a go

The names of these occupations are in alphabetical order.

Tick ☑ the correct definition. Use a dictionary to help you.

astronaut
- looks after passengers on an aircraft ☐
- travels in space in a spaceship ☐

chef
- a cook in a hotel or restaurant ☐
- someone paid to drive a car ☐

diver
- works underwater ☐
- drives a car, bus, lorry or train ☐

editor
- repairs many kinds of electrical things ☐
- someone in charge of a newspaper ☐

florist
- sells flowers and plants ☐
- puts out fires ☐

joiner
- does clever tricks throwing and catching things ☐
- makes things out of wood ☐

mason
- works underground digging up coal ☐
- carves and builds with stone ☐

newsagent
- sells newspapers and magazines ☐
- reads the news on radio or TV ☐

surgeon
- doctor who performs operations ☐
- works in an office ☐

Unit 29: Rhyming (2)

Remember

We must **listen** carefully to identify words that **rhyme**.
We also need to **look** carefully.
Some **rhyming words** contain the **same letter patterns**.

I will t**ry** not to c**ry**.

Have a go

Make some rhyming words. Read the words you make.

a Change the **c** in **c**are to **d**, **sh**, **sc**, **st**, **squ**.

dare ____ share ____ scare ____ stare ____ square ____

b Change the **p** in **p**art to **c**, **d**, **t**, **st**, **ch**.

______ ______ ______ ______ ______

c Change the **f** in **f**ear to **n**, **d**, **h**, **cl**, **sp**.

______ ______ ______ ______ ______

d Change the **h** in **h**orn to **b**, **c**, **t**, **w**, **forl**.

______ ______ ______ ______ ______

e Change the **t** in **t**own to **d**, **g**, **br**, **dr**, **fr**.

______ ______ ______ ______ ______

f Change the **p** in **p**age to **c**, **r**, **w**.

______ ______ ______

g Change the **d** in **d**ance to **l**, **pr**, **ch**, **gl**.

______ ______ ______ ______

Unit 30: Prefixes – *re* and *pre*

Remember

A **prefix** is a **group of letters** we add on to the **front** of a word.
Prefixes change the **meaning** of the word.

re + fill = refill

The prefix **re** means 'to do again'.

pre + fix = prefix

Pre means 'before' or 'in front of'.

Have a go

1 Write these words as word sums. Read the words you make.

a prefix = pre + fix
b preheat = ______ + ______
c preface = ______ + ______
d prepaid = ______ + ______
e premature = ______ + ______
f rebuild = ______ + ______
g retake = ______ + ______
h replace = ______ + ______
i replay = ______ + ______
j refill = ______ + ______

2 Use the words above to fill the gaps in the sentences.

a The baby was born too soon. It was ______.
b The jug was empty so I had to ______ it.
c We did not have to put a stamp on the letter because it was ______.
d A ______ goes at the front of a book.
e When something is worn out you have to ______ it.
f A ______ is a group of letters that may be added to the beginning of a word.
g As the game was rained off we had to ______ it.
h The wall fell down so my dad had to ______ it.
i ______ the milk before you add the custard powder.
j I failed my test so I had to ______ it.

Unit 31: Using adjectives (2)

Remember

An **adjective** is a **describing** word.
An adjective gives us more **information about a noun**.

a **clever** puppy

Have a go

1 Choose the most suitable adjective to describe each animal.

sly gentle wise strong quiet busy slippery playful

a as ________ as a mouse

b as ________ as a bee

c as ________ as a dove

d as ________ as an ox

e as ________ as an eel

f as ________ as an owl

g as ________ as a fox

h as ________ as a kitten

2 Find and circle the eight adjectives in this puzzle.

a	b	s	c	a	r	y	c
f	u	n	n	y	d	e	f
g	h	i	h	e	a	v	y
j	m	o	d	e	r	n	k
o	p	e	n	o	p	q	r
s	t	w	d	e	e	p	x
w	i	d	e	z	y	v	s
b	n	s	m	o	o	t	h

Unit 32: Silent letters – *b* and *g*

Remember

Some words contain **silent letters**.
We cannot hear them when we say the words.

lam**b** 

gnome 

Have a go

1 Choose **b** or **g** to complete each word. Read the words you make.

lam__ **__naw** **com__** **__nash** **thum__**

__nat **crum__** **__nome** **clim__** **__narled**

2 Complete this chart with the words you made:

words ending with a silent **b**	words beginning with a silent **g**

3 Use the words to complete these sentences.

a Your ________ is part of your hand.

b A baby sheep is called a ________.

c A _______ is a kind of goblin.

d A _______ is a small flying insect.

e You _______ your hair.

f A ________ is a small piece of bread.

g A dog will ________ a bone.

h You ________ your teeth when you are angry.

i ________ means twisted and knobbly.

j You _______ a mountain.

Unit 33: Suffixes – *er*

Remember

A **suffix** is a **group of letters** we add to the **end** of a word.
A suffix changes the **meaning** of the word.
We can change some **verbs** into **nouns** by adding the suffix **er**.

sing + **er** = singer
(verb) (noun)

dance + **er** = dancer
(verb) (noun)

Have a go

1 Add **er** to each verb to make some nouns. Read the words that you make.

a reporter**er**	b build__	c climb__	d garden__	e teach__
reporter	______	______	______	______
f football__	g paint__	h clean__	i box__	j farm__
______	______	______	______	______

2 Write the correct noun under each picture.

a  ______

b  ______

c  ______

d  ______

e  ______

f  ______

g  ______

h  ______

i  ______

j  ______

3 Add the suffix **er** to each of these verbs. Take care with the spelling!

a drum ______	b skate ______	c ride ______
d write ______	e swim ______	f shop ______
g drive ______	h win ______	i run ______

Unit 34: Using apostrophes (2)

Remember

We can **shorten** some words by missing some letters out.

We put an **apostrophe** to show where letters are missing.

it's = it is   can't = cannot

Have a go

Set A

isn't | wasn't | doesn't | wouldn't | won't

you're | he's | it's | they're | I've | I'm

they've | we'll | she'll | who's | that's

Set B

you are | would not | they are | we will | does not

is not | it is | I am | who is | will not | I have

he is | that is | was not | she will | they have

Match up the longer and shorter forms that mean the same from Set A and Set B. Write them here:

isn't = is not   ______ = ______   ______ = ______

______ = ______   ______ = ______   ______ = ______

______ = ______   ______ = ______   ______ = ______

______ = ______   ______ = ______   ______ = ______

______ = ______   ______ = ______

______ = ______   ______ = ______

Unit 35: Singular and plural (2)

Remember

Singular means **one**. **Plural** means **more than one**.

one monk**ey**

two monkey**s**

one ba**by**

two bab**ies**

When a word ends with
a **vowel** + **y**
we just add **s** to make it plural.

When a word ends with
a **consonant** + **y**
we change the **y** to **i** and add **es**.

Have a go

1 Write the plural of these words:

a ray ________ b turkey ____________ c boy __________

d guy ________ e monkey __________ f holiday ___________

g donkey _________ h valley __________ i chimney __________

j jockey __________ k tray _________ l display ___________

2 Fill in the plural form of each noun in the gaps.

a Two _________ (lorry) crashed on the motorway.

b Some _________ (lady) wear yellow hats.

c We ate all the _________ (cherry) in the bowl.

d I had three _________ (reply) to my advertisement.

e There were two _________ (baby) in the pram.

f James scored three _________ (try) in rugby.

g I hate _________ (fly)!

h I heard some _________ (cry) coming from the cellar.

Unit 36: Possessive pronouns

Remember

A **pronoun** is a word that **takes the place of a noun**.
Possessive pronouns tell us who something **belongs to**.

This is my ball not **yours**!

No! The ball is **mine**!

Here are all the **possessive pronouns**.

mine yours his hers its ours theirs

Have a go

1 Circle the possessive pronouns in these sentences.

a This coat is mine.

b The children picked up the bags that were theirs.

c Sue did not think Anna's dress was as nice as hers.

d When Tom looked closely he saw that the book was not his.

e "Is this pen yours?" Mrs Shah asked Tom.

f The boys looked at the painting and said, "Ours is the best!"

2 Choose the correct possessive pronoun to go in each gap.

a This is my toy. It's ________ (mine, yours).

b The girl was sure the pen was ________ (its, hers).

c The muddy trainers belonged to Tom and Ben. They were ________ (his, theirs).

d "You can't have the ball. It's ________ (yours, ours)!" shouted Luke.

e "Are these your sweets?" the teacher asked Amy. "Yes. They are ________ (hers, mine)," she replied.

f This coat belongs to you. It is ________ (theirs, yours).

Unit 37: Subject and verb agreement (2)

Remember

Every sentence must have a **verb**.
Every verb must have a **subject** (the person or thing that goes with the verb).
The subject and verb must always **agree**.

The birds was making a nest. ☒  The birds were making a nest. ☑

Have a go

1. Choose 'was' or 'were' to complete each sentence.

a All of the puppies ______ asleep.
b The girls ______ laughing.
c A frog ______ hopping along.
d Some ants ______ running around.
e Each bike ______ new.
f That red car ______ going too fast.
g Lots of children ______ shouting.
h A monkey ______ eating a banana.

2. Rewrite each sentence correctly.

a There were a storm and some children was nervous.

____

b While the men was fishing I were looking for sea shells.

____

c It were hot as we was playing cricket.

____

d I were reading while you was writing.

____

e We was worried because our mum were not well.

____

f My friends was happy but I were sad.

____

Unit 38: Using conjunctions

Remember

A **conjunction** is a **joining** word. We use a **conjunction** to join two short sentences together to make one longer sentence.

Tom whistled. He went to school. Tom whistled **as** he went to school.

Have a go

1. Underline the conjunction in each long sentence below.

   a Mrs Smith came into the room and Ben followed her.

   b The red parrot squawked but the blue parrot stayed silent.

   c Vicky was good at maths but she was no good at sport.

   d I cut the bread and made a sandwich.

   e We went to the cinema and saw a very good film.

   f My trainers were cheap but my new jeans were expensive.

   g Sharon decided to walk to town but it began to rain.

2. Now rewrite each long sentence as two short sentences.

   a **Mrs Smith came into the room. Ben followed her.**

   b ______________________________

   c ______________________________

   d ______________________________

   e ______________________________

   f ______________________________

   g ______________________________

Unit 39: Synonyms

Remember

Synonyms are words that have **similar meanings**.

sleep doze slumber

Have a go

1 Complete each sentence with the verb from the box which has the same meaning as the verb in brackets.

baked cuddled found cleaned bumped jumped mended grinned

a I (discovered) ______________ some hidden treasure.

b I (cooked) ______________ a loaf of bread.

c I (washed) ______________ the car.

d I (leapt) ______________ over the wall.

e I (banged) ______________ my knee.

f I (fixed) ______________ the broken toy.

g I (hugged) ______________ my best friend.

h I (smiled) ______________ at my aunt.

2 Think of a verb with a similar meaning to the verb in brackets.

a I (tore) ______________ my trousers.

b The man (dozed) ______________ in bed.

c The police officer (seized) ______________ the thief.

d We (defeated) ______________ the other football team.

e The girl (shouted) ______________ at the top of her voice.

f The boy (constructed) ______________ a lovely model aeroplane.

g The children (raced) ______________ to the finishing post.

h Sam (giggled) ______________ at the funny film.

Unit 40: Using speech marks (2)

Remember

The words people actually say go inside **speech marks**.
We begin the **first** word inside the speech marks with a **capital letter**.

The hare said, "Let's have a race."

Have a go

Write these sentences correctly.

a The hare said, let's have a race.

The hare said, "Let's have a race."

b The tortoise said, ready, steady, go!

____

c i can run faster than you, the hare said.

____

d The tortoise said, i can only walk slowly.

____

e The hare said, as the tortoise is so slow I can have a sleep!

____

f The tortoise said, now he is asleep I can pass the hare.

____

g The hare shouted, oh no! the tortoise is at the winning post!

____

h I'm the winner! the tortoise shouted happily.

____

Test 1

Check how much you have learned.

Answer the questions.
Mark your answers. Fill in your score.

SCORE

1. Write these sentences correctly.

   a a girl is swimming ______________________________

   b some boys are playing __________________________

   out of 2 ☐

2. Do these phoneme sums.

   a s + l + ee + p = _______

   b t + or + ch = _______

   out of 2 ☐

3. Fill in the missing nouns.

   a A d_________ looks after our teeth.

   b A c_________ tells us the time.

   out of 2 ☐

4. Fill in the missing commas.

   a In my bag I have a book a pen a ruler and a pencil.

   b March April May and June are months of the year.

   out of 2 ☐

5. Complete these words.

   a

   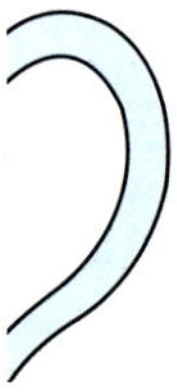

   hand___

   b

   eag___

   out of 2 ☐

6 The two compound words have got mixed up. Write them correctly.

a

windball

____

b

footmill

____

out of 2

7 Fill in the correct form of each verb.

a I am ____________ (wink) my eye.

b I am ____________ (hum) a tune.

out of 2

8 Write each set of words in alphabetical order.

a carrot apple date beetroot

________ ________ ________ ________

b snow sack slide skin

________ ________ ________ ________

out of 2

9 Underline the pair of rhyming words in each set.

a head good need bread

b kind round found grow

out of 2

10 Choose **un** or **dis** to complete each word.

a ______agree b ____lucky

out of 2

Total out of 20

Test 2

Check how much you have learned.

Answer the questions.
Mark your answers. Fill in your score.

SCORE

1 Choose the best adjective for each gap.

a a ______________ (wide, beautiful) princess

b a ______________ (tall, hot) tower

out of 2

2 Choose **k** or **w** to begin each word.

a

___rist

b

___nee

out of 2

3 Take the suffix off each word. Write the words that are left.

a helpful _________ b restless _________

out of 2

4 Write the longer forms of these words.

a you're ___________ b don't ___________

out of 2

5 Fill in the missing plurals.

a one box lots of _____________

b one arch several _____________

out of 2

6 Choose the correct pronoun for each gap.

a When the girl sat down ______ (he, she) read a book.

b I saw the boy but ______ (he, she) didn't see me.

out of 2

7 Choose the correct verb.

a A horse ________ (neigh, neighs).

b Some snakes _______ (hiss, hisses).

out of 2

8 Underline the conjunction in each sentence.

a I got undressed and I went to bed.

b I tried to sleep but I could not.

out of 2

9 Underline the pair of synonyms in each set.

a speak look talk open

b write answer reply sing

out of 2

10 Fill in the missing speech marks.

a Jack said, Have you seen my bag?

b Sarah said, It is by your chair.

out of 2

Total out of 20

Test 3

Check how much you have learned.

Answer the questions.
Mark your answers. Fill in your score.

SCORE

1 Write each question correctly.

a what is the weather like ______________________

b is it raining ______________________

out of 2

2 Fill in the missing phoneme in each word.

a

c___t

b

c___ch

out of 2

3 Write each proper noun correctly.

a wednesday ______________________

b october ______________________

out of 2

4 Fill in the missing comma in each sentence.

a

b

out of 2

5 Complete the missing words.

a The opposite of day is n_______.

b When it is dark I switch on the l_______.

out of 2

6 The two compound words have got mixed up. Write them correctly.

a

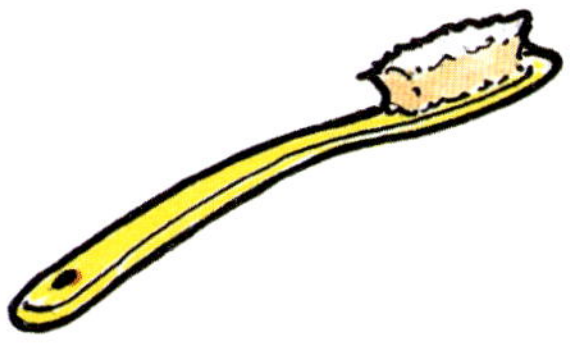

handbrush

______

b

toothbag

______

out of 2

7 Fill in the correct form of each verb.

a Yesterday I ______ (walk) to town.

b Last week I ______ (slip) over.

out of 2

8 Complete each definition.

a The g______ is the largest and strongest kind of ape.

b A p______ is used to keep the water in a sink or bath.

out of 2

9 Underline the pair of rhyming words in each set.

a **cry** **fear** **torn** **near**

b **dance** **town** **chance** **part**

out of 2

10 Choose **re** or **pre** to begin each word.

a ___place

b ____historic

out of 2

Total out of 20

Test 4

Check how much you have learned.

Answer the questions.
Mark your answers. Fill in your score.

SCORE

1 Choose the most sensible adjective for each gap.

a as ___________ (gentle, fierce) as a lion

b as ___________ (slow, fast) as a snail

out of 2

2 Choose **b** or **g** to complete each word.

a

__nome

b

thum__

out of 2

3 Add the suffix **er** to each word. Write each word correctly.

a

build + er

____

b

football + er

____

out of 2

4 Write the longer forms of the underlined words.

a I can't do it. I ___________ do it.

b You're a clever child. _______ ______ a clever child.

out of 2

5 Fill in the correct form of the plural.

a There were two ___________ (monkey) in the tree.

b Some ___________ (baby) cry a lot.

out of 2

6 Underline the possessive pronouns in each sentence.

a Is this bag yours?

b The ball is mine.

7 Write **was** or **were** in each gap.

a Some cows _______ mooing.

b The sun _______ shining.

8 Underline the conjunction in each sentence.

a The wind blew and the rain fell.

b I can hop but I can't skip.

9 Underline the pair of synonyms in each set.

a **discover** **climb** **find** **rest**

b **write** **shut** **call** **close**

10 Write these sentences correctly.

a Anna said do you want an apple?

____

b Ben said may I have a banana instead?

____

out of 2

out of 2

out of 2

out of 2

out of 2

Total out of 20

Parents' notes

Unit 1: Full stops and capital letters Punctuation marks tell the reader how to read a text. All sentences should begin with a capital letter. Most sentences end with a full stop. Full stops help break the text up and help the reader make sense of it.

Unit 2: Word-building with phonemes All words are made up of phonemes (units of sound). Sometimes phonemes may be single letters. Sometimes they consist of two or more letters which make one sound e.g. **ou** and **ow**. Your child needs to know how to build up words using phonemes.

Unit 3: Nouns All words may be classified according to the jobs they do in sentences. Nouns (naming words) play an essential part in grammar. Nouns may be the names of people, places or things.

Unit 4: Commas in lists We use commas to separate items in a list. Commas are a signal to the reader to pause briefly. Usually we do not use a comma before the word 'and'.

Unit 5: Letter patterns – *le* There are many common letter patterns (letters which frequently come together) in words. It is important for your child to recognise these when reading and to be able to use them when writing.

Unit 6: Compound words (1) Compound words are words that are made by joining two smaller words together to make one longer word. A useful spelling strategy to learn is to look for smaller words 'hiding' inside longer words.

Unit 7: Verbs – present tense All words may be classified according to the jobs they do in sentences. Verbs (doing words) play an essential part in grammar. When the verb tells of an action taking place now, we say that it is written in the present tense. There are two forms of the present tense – the simple present (e.g. I swim) and the present continuous (e.g. I am swimming).

Unit 8: Alphabetical order A dictionary is a very valuable tool for a child. Your child needs to know how to use one. This unit focuses on understanding alphabetical order, according to the first and second letters of words.

Unit 9: Rhyming (1) Rhyming involves good listening skills. The ability to differentiate and hear differences in sounds and rhymes is an important early reading and spelling skill. In the activity in this unit, the rhyming parts of the pairs of words sound and look similar.

Unit 10: Prefixes *un* and *dis* Remind your child that a prefix is a group of letters we can add to the front of a word. Prefixes change the meaning of the word. The addition of the prefix **un** or **dis** gives the word the opposite meaning e.g. well – unwell. Note that the spelling of the original word is never changed when a prefix is added.

Unit 11: Using adjectives (1) An adjective is a describing word. It tells us more about a noun. Adjectives help us make our writing more interesting and descriptive.

Unit 12: Silent letters – *k* and *w* Some words contain silent letters. We can't hear these when we say the words. Point out to your child that the silent **k** is always followed by **n**, and the silent **w** is always followed by **r**, in the words.

Unit 13: Suffixes – *ful* and *less* A suffix is a group of letters we add to the end of a word. Your child needs to understand that many words may be extended by adding suffixes. Adding a suffix changes the meaning of the word in some way. In this unit the suffixes **ful** and **less** are added to words to give them the opposite meanings.

Unit 14: Using apostrophes (1) We sometimes shorten words and miss out letters. These words are called contractions. (To 'contract' means to make shorter.) We use an apostrophe to show where letters are missing. We use contractions a lot in spoken language but less so in written language.

Unit 15: Singular and plural (1) Nouns may be singular (when there is only one) or plural (when there is more than one). The most common way to make a noun plural is to add **s** (as in 'trees'). However, sometimes the spelling of the plural noun is made by adding **es** (as in the examples in this unit).

Unit 16: Personal pronouns A pronoun is a word that takes the place of a noun. ('Pro' actually means 'in place of'.) We use pronouns to avoid a lot of repetition in sentences. Personal pronouns take the place of the names of people or things e.g. Tom bought a comic when he (Tom) went out.

Unit 17: Subject and verb agreement (1) When children are writing, very often their minds go faster than their pens. One common mistake is for the verb in the sentence not to agree with the subject (the main thing or person) in the sentence.

Unit 18: Conjunctions – *and* and *but* A conjunction is a joining word which may be used to join two sentences together. (Your child may be helped to remember this by likening it to a road junction, where two roads join together.) Two common conjunctions are the words **and** and **but**.

Unit 19: Words with similar meanings Synonyms are words which have the same, or very similar meanings. Using synonyms makes our writing more interesting and adds variety. Encourage your child to use a thesaurus if you have one.

Unit 20: Using speech marks (1) When we write down what people say, we use speech marks. Remind your child that the words a person says should go inside the speech marks.

Unit 21: Using question marks Remind your child that all sentences should begin with a capital letter, and that most sentences end with a full stop. However, when a question is being asked, the sentence must end with a question mark.

Unit 22: Finding the missing phonemes Encourage your child to say the name of each picture aloud and to listen for the missing phoneme. An important skill your child needs to know is how to build up words using phonemes.

Unit 23: Proper nouns Common nouns were revised in Unit 3. In this unit the focus is proper nouns. A proper noun is the particular name of a person, place or thing. Proper nouns always begin with a capital letter.

Unit 24: Commas in sentences Commas are used to separate any extra bits that are added to the beginning or ending of a sentence e.g. Come here, Sam. Commas are a signal to the reader to pause briefly.

Unit 25: Letter patterns – *igh* Remind your child that there are many common letter patterns (letters which frequently come together) in words. The letter pattern **igh** is the focus of this unit.

Unit 26: Compound words (2) Compound words (words that are made by joining two smaller words together to make one longer word) were revised in Unit 6. In this unit your child is encouraged to use picture clues to make some common compound words.

Unit 27: Verbs – past tense Verbs (doing words) in the present tense were revised in Unit 7. In this unit verbs in the past tense are revised. When the verb tells of an action which took place in the past, we say that it is written in the past tense. The past tense of many verbs is formed by adding **ed**. (Note that sometimes this changes the spelling of the original verb slightly.)

Unit 28: Dictionary work – definitions It is important that your child understands how to use a dictionary. This unit focuses on its function of supplying definitions of words.

Unit 29: Rhyming (2) In the activity in this unit, your child changes the letters in words to make other rhyming words.

Unit 30: Prefixes – *re* and *pre* The prefixes **un** and **dis** were revised in Unit 10. This unit focuses on the prefixes **re** (meaning 'to do again') and **pre** (meaning 'before' or 'in front of'). Note that the spelling of the original word is never changed when a prefix is added.

Unit 31: Using adjectives (2) The use of adjectives (describing words) was revised in Unit 11. In this unit this focus is extended.

Unit 32: Silent letters – *b* and *g* Encourage your child to read the words containing silent letters. Note how the silent **b** is always preceded by **m**, and the silent **g** is always followed by **n**, in the words.

Unit 33: Suffixes – *er* The suffixes **ful** and **less** were revised in Unit 13. (A suffix is a group of letters we add to the end of a word.) Adding a suffix changes the meaning of the word in some way. In this unit verbs are changed into nouns by adding the suffix **er**.

Unit 34: Using apostrophes (2) The use of apostrophes (to shorten words and show where letters are missing) was revisited in Unit 14. More contractions using apostrophes are revised in this unit.

Unit 35: Singular and plural (2) Remind your child that nouns may be singular (when there is only one) or plural (when there is more than one). The most common way to make a noun plural is to add **s** (as in words ending with a vowel + **y** e.g. 'toys'). However, when the word ends in a consonant + y, we have to change the **y** to **i**, and add **es**.

Unit 36: Possessive pronouns Remind your child that a pronoun is a word that takes the place of a noun. ('Pro' actually means 'in place of'.) The focus of this unit is possessive pronouns.

Unit 37: Subject and verb agreement (2) Subject and verb agreement was revised in Unit 17. This unit offers some further revision.

Unit 38: Using conjunctions Remind your child that a conjunction is a joining word which may be used to join two sentences together. This unit extends the work on conjunctions introduced in Unit 18.

Unit 39: Synonyms This unit offers further revision of synonyms. (These are words which have the same, or very similar meanings.) Encourage your child to use a thesaurus if you have one.

Unit 40: Using speech marks (2) Your child needs to know how to write dialogue (what people say). Remind your child that the words a person says should go inside speech marks. Note that the first word inside the speech marks usually begins with a capital letter, since this is the first word of the sentence the person is actually saying.

Answers

Unit 1: Full stops and capital letters (page 6)

1
- a The sun is shining.
- b The sky is blue.
- c There are some clouds.
- d It is very hot.
- e We are going to the park.
- f In the park there is a lake.

2
- a The driver stopped the bus. The boy got off.
- b The woman came home from the shop. She had some apples in her bag.
- c The firefighters stopped at the fire. They soon put it out.
- d The boy liked his baby sister. Sometimes she smiled at him.
- e The bird built a nest. It laid several eggs in it.

Unit 2: Word-building with phonemes (page 7)

1
- a sheep
- b boat
- c chart
- d dream
- e play
- f road
- g toy
- h grow
- i loud
- j join

2
- a foot
- b cow
- c girl
- d purse
- e play
- f nail
- g seat
- h claw
- i glue
- j snow

Unit 3: Nouns (page 8)

1
- a detective
- b plumber
- c hospital
- d museum
- e staple
- f fence

2
- a vegetables
- b sports
- c musical instruments
- d fruits
- e things for writing with
- f clothes
- g cutlery
- h means of transport

Unit 4: Commas in lists (page 9)

1
- a Sunday, Monday, Tuesday and Wednesday are days of the week.
- b For my birthday I had some paints, a book, a game and a jigsaw.
- c A gardener needs a rake, a spade, a fork and some shears.
- d Sarah has a thin face, black hair, brown eyes and a small nose.
- e On holiday I visited France, Germany, Italy and Spain.
- f In the woods I saw a fox, a squirrel, some birds and a hedgehog.

2 Check that the answers show the correct use of commas.

Unit 5: Letter patterns – *le* (page 10)

1
- a handle, needle, middle, ladle, cradle
- b angle, single, eagle, jingle, jungle

2

ble words	fle words	kle words	ple words	tle words
grumble	rifle	sparkle	purple	title
table	trifle	tickle	simple	battle
feeble	raffle	ankle	example	
	muffle			

Unit 6: Compound words (1) (page 11)

handwriting
bathroom
birthday
pancake
sunshine
someone
nobody
windmill
bookcase
footstep
blackbird
carpet
anyway

Unit 7: Verbs – present tense (page 12)

1. a I am jumping.
   b I am **catching**.
   c I am **cooking**.
   d I am **speaking**.
   e I am **walking**.
   f I am **singing**.
   g I am **looking**.
   h I am **drawing**.

2. a swimming b hopping
   c driving d baking
   e wagging f skipping
   g smiling h shining
   i biting j clapping

Unit 8: Alphabetical order (page 13)

1. a antelope bat cat donkey
   b giraffe leopard mouse panda tiger

2. a hamster hedgehog hippo horse
   b camel cheetah cow crocodile
   c rabbit reindeer rhino rook
   d panda pelican pig pony puppy
   e octopus orangutan ostrich owl ox

Unit 9: Rhyming (1) (page 14)

choice	voice
fire	wire
found	round
hedge	ledge
bread	tread
piece	niece
claw	paw
dear	near
carry	marry
spice	twice

Unit 10: Prefixes *un* and *dis* (page 15)

1. a **un**well b **dis**agree
   c **dis**appear d **un**lucky
   e **un**comfortable f **dis**obedient
   g **un**lock h **dis**appoint
   i **dis**honest j **un**pack

2. a Sam **un**locked her suitcase.
   b The two children always **dis**agreed with each other.
   c I feel very **un**lucky today.
   d My dog is very **dis**obedient.
   e The man was very **dis**honest.
   f The sports car **dis**appeared in a flash.
   g Tom looked rather **un**well.
   h The armchair was very **un**comfortable.
   i Ben **un**packed the shopping in the trolley.
   j I **dis**like sprouts very much.

Unit 11: Using adjectives (1) (page 16)

1. a a crunchy apple
   b an exciting story
   c the old lady
   d a windy day
   e some ripe bananas
   f a tiny baby
   g some buzzing bees
   h an angry bull
   i a beautiful hat
   j some golden sand
   k the blunt pencil
   l a tall building

2. a loud b heavy
   c dirty d fizzy
   e empty f handsome
   g straight h rough

Unit 12: Silent letters – *k* and *w* (page 17)

1 a knot, know, knee, knife, knock
b wrap, wreck, wrist, write, wrong

2 wreck, know, knot, knock, wrist, knife, wrap, write, knee, wrong

Unit 13: Suffixes – *ful* and *less* (page 18)

1 a helpful, helpless
b thoughtful, thoughtless
c painful, painless
d colourful, colourless
e hopeful, hopeless
f powerful, powerless
g useful, useless
h restful, restless
i thankful, thankless
j harmful, harmless

2 a pity
b success
c mercy
d speech
e respect
f mind
g friend
h wonder
i beauty
j sense

Unit 14: Using apostrophes (1) (page 19)

1
I'm	I am
we've	we have
they're	they are
she's	she is
wouldn't	would not
they'll	they will
you're	you are
it's	it is
wasn't	was not
doesn't	does not

2 a wouldn't
b they're
c we've
d I'm
e you're
f she's
g wasn't
h they'll
i doesn't

Unit 15: Singular and plural (1) (page 20)

singular	plural
one fox	lots of **foxes**
one kiss	lots of **kisses**
one **church**	lots of churches
one **dish**	lots of dishes
one box	lots of **boxes**
one **glass**	lots of glasses
one **bus**	lots of buses
one wish	lots of **wishes**
one **match**	lots of matches
one arch	lots of **arches**
one brush	lots of **brushes**
one **stitch**	lots of stitches

Unit 16: Personal pronouns (page 21)

1 a I love strawberries.
b We are going to the park.
c Can you swim?
d The girl cried when she fell over.
e The old man sat down because he was tired.
f The police caught the men and put them in jail.
g I threw a stick and the dog picked it up.

2 a she b you c It d they
e I f he/me

Unit 17: Subject and verb agreement (1) (page 22)

1 a Birds sing.
b A horse gallops.
c The snake hisses.

d Some children **giggle**.
e Emma **is running**.
f The baby **smiled**.
g A telephone **rings**.
h My dad **snores**.

2 a quacks b hoot c go
d do e have f moves
g roar h moos

Unit 18: Conjunctions – *and* and *but* (page 23)

1 a The alien opened its mouth and it began to speak.
b Edward called for Sam and they went to the park.
c Lucy went to bed and she read a book.
d The spider spun a web and it caught a fly.
e Tom got some seeds and he planted them in the garden.

2 a Kate loves chips but Emma hates them.
b I tried the key but it would not open the door.
c My dog loves walks but it does not like having a bath.
d The car went fast but it made a lot of noise.

Unit 19: Words with similar meanings (page 24)

sweep	brush
eat	chew
cry	sob
shut	close
run	race
speak	talk
moan	groan
grab	grasp
reply	answer
open	unlock
chew	bite
begin	start
end	finish

Unit 20: Using speech marks (2) (page 25)

1 a Emma said, "I like skating."
b Ben said, "Let's play a video game."
c Edward said, "I want to go for a bike ride."
d Anna asked, "What is for dinner?"
e Ali asked, "Where is Tom?"
f Sarah said, "Pass me my bag, please."
g Nicky exclaimed, "What a lovely present!"
h Rehannah shouted, "Look at this!"

2 a Neigh b Quack c Hiss
d Gobble e Woof f Buzz
g Squeak h Baa

Unit 21: Using question marks (page 26)

1 a What is your name?
b Where do you live?
c How old are you?
d When is your birthday?
e Which school do you go to?

2 The answers below are examples only. Other answers are possible.
a What is the time?
b What is the capital of France?
c What would you like to eat?
d Who is Mrs Smith?
e Where is my pen?
f What is your favourite colour?
g Where are you going on holiday this year?
h Who is that present for?

Unit 22: Finding the missing phonemes (page 27)

a bird
b coach
c grass
d chair
e draw
f book
g mouth
h torch
i coin
j crown
k church
l shark

Unit 23: Proper nouns (page 28)

1
a Edinburgh
b Amy
c Wednesday
d Ford Road
e King Henry
f Daily Mail
g Rome
h April
i Humpty Dumpty
j Newcastle United

2
a Mrs Brown is my teacher.
b On holiday Sarah visited Paris in France.
c Last Thursday Jamie went to see London Bridge.
d Mrs Shah was reading the Daily Telegraph.
e We are staying in the Grand Hotel in Dover.
f The plane from Mumbai landed at Gatwick Airport.

Unit 24: Commas in sentences (page 29)

1
a Sam, come here.
b Where are you, Mum?
c May I have an apple, please?
d Dad, look at me!
e Sorry, Miss.
f What's the matter, Mr Jordan?
g Sarah, stop pushing me.
h I can't do it, can I?
i Ben, stop at once!
j I'll go to bed, shall I?

2
a May I have a drink, please?
b No, you can't.
c Tom, pass me my bag.
d Yes, here it is.
e Sam, would you like a cake?
f I would like a doughnut, I think.
g Stop cheating, Jo.
h That's not fair, Mum.

Unit 25: Letter patterns – *igh* (page 30)

1 high thigh sigh
right night fight light might
sight tight

2 high sigh thigh

3 fight light might night right
sight tight

4
a tight
b high/sight
c right
d night
e might/light

Unit 26: Compound words (2) (page 31)

a ladybird
b handbag
c horseshoe
d sheepdog
e butterfly
f toothbrush
g pancake
h snowball
i sunlight
j footpath

Unit 27: Verbs – past tense (page 32)

1

Present tense	Past tense
Today I splash.	Yesterday I splashed.
Today I jump.	Yesterday I **jumped**.
Today I play.	Yesterday I **played**.
Today I walk.	Yesterday I **walked**.
Today I paint.	Yesterday I **painted**.
Today I help.	Yesterday I **helped**.

2
a hopped
b ripped
c smiled
d tried
e snored
f sobbed

Unit 28: Dictionary work – definitions (page 33)

astronaut travels in space in a spaceship √

chef	a cook in a hotel or restaurant √
diver	works underwater √
editor	someone in charge of a newspaper √
florist	sells flowers and plants √
joiner	makes things out of wood √
mason	carves and builds with stone √
newsagent	sells newspapers and magazines √
surgeon	doctor who performs operations √

Unit 29: Rhyming (2) (page 34)

a dare share scare stare square
b cart dart tart start chart
c near dear hear clear spear
d born corn torn worn forlorn
e down gown brown drown frown
f cage rage wage
g lance prance chance glance

Unit 30: Prefixes – *re* and *pre* (page 35)

1 a pre + fix b pre + heat
c pre + face d pre + paid
e pre + mature f re + build
g re + take h re + place
i re + play j re + fill

2 a premature b refill
c prepaid d preface
e replace f prefix
g replay h rebuild
i preheat j retake

Unit 31: Using adjectives (2) (page 36)

1 a quiet b busy c gentle
d strong e slippery f wise
g sly h playful

2

a	b	s	c	a	r	y	c
f	u	n	n	y	d	e	f
g	h	i	h	e	a	v	y
j	m	o	d	e	r	n	k
o	p	e	n	o	p	q	r
s	t	w	d	e	e	p	x
w	i	d	e	z	y	v	s
b	n	s	m	o	o	t	h

Unit 32: Silent letters – *b* and *g* (page 37)

1 lam**b** **g**naw com**b** **g**nash
thum**b** **g**nat crum**b** **g**nome
clim**b** **g**narled

2

words ending with a silent **b**	words beginning with a silent **g**
lamb comb thumb crumb climb	gnaw gnash gnat gnome gnarled

3 a thumb b lamb
c gnome d gnat
e comb f crumb
g gnaw h gnash
i Gnarled j climb

Unit 33: Suffixes – *er* (page 38)

1 a report**er** b build**er**
c climb**er** d garden**er**
e teach**er** f football**er**
g paint**er** h clean**er**
i box**er** j farm**er**

2 a climber b builder
c boxer d farmer
e teacher f painter

g gardener h reporter
i cleaner j footballer

3 a drummer b skater
c rider d writer
e swimmer f shopper
g driver h winner
i runner

Unit 34: Using apostrophes (2) (page 39)

isn't	=	is not
wasn't	=	was not
doesn't	=	does not
wouldn't	=	would not
won't	=	will not
you're	=	you are
he's	=	he is
it's	=	it is
they're	=	they are
I've	=	I have
I'm	=	I am
they've	=	they have
we'll	=	we will
she'll	=	she will
who's	=	who is
that's	=	that is

Unit 35: Singular and plural (2) (page 40)

1 a rays b turkeys
c boys d guys
e monkeys f holidays
g donkeys h valleys
i chimneys j jockeys
k trays l displays

2 a lorries b ladies
c cherries d replies
e babies f tries
g flies h cries

Unit 36: Possessive pronouns (page 41)

1 a This coat is **mine**.
b The children picked up the bags that were **theirs**.
c Sue did not think Anna's dress was as nice as **hers**.
d When Tom looked closely he saw that the book was not **his**.
e "Is this pen **yours**?" Mrs Shah asked Tom.
f The boys looked at the painting and said, "**Ours** is the best!"

2 a This is my toy. It's mine.
b The girl was sure the pen was hers.
c The muddy trainers belonged to Tom and Ben. They were theirs.
d "You can't have the ball. It's ours!" shouted Luke.
e "Are these your sweets?" the teacher asked Amy. "Yes. They are mine," she replied.
f This coat belongs to you. It is yours.

Unit 37: Subject and verb agreement (2) (page 42)

1 a were b were c was
d were e was f was
g were h was

2 a There was a storm and some children were nervous.
b While the men were fishing I was looking for sea shells.
c It was hot as we were playing cricket.
d I was reading while you were writing.
e We were worried because our mum was not well.
f My friends were happy but I was sad.

Unit 38: Using conjunctions (page 43)

1. a Mrs Smith came into the room and Ben followed her.
   b The red parrot squawked but the blue parrot stayed silent.
   c Vicky was good at maths but she was no good at sport.
   d I cut the bread and made a sandwich.
   e We went to the cinema and saw a very good film.
   f My trainers were cheap but my new jeans were expensive.
   g Sharon decided to walk to town but it began to rain.

2. a Mrs Smith came into the room. Ben followed her.
   b The red parrot squawked. The blue parrot stayed silent.
   c Vicky was good at maths. She was no good at sport.
   d I cut the bread. I made a sandwich.
   e We went to the cinema. We saw a very good film.
   f My trainers were cheap. My new jeans were expensive.
   g Sharon decided to walk to town. It began to rain.

Unit 39: Synonyms (page 44)

1. a found b baked
   c cleaned d jumped
   e bumped f mended
   g cuddled h grinned

2. The answers given are examples only. Other answers are possible.
   a ripped b slept
   c caught d beat
   e yelled f built
   g ran h laughed

Unit 40: Using speech marks (2) (page 45)

a The hare said, "Let's have a race."
b The tortoise said, "Ready, steady, go!"
c "I can run faster than you," the hare said.
d The tortoise said, "I can only walk slowly."
e The hare said, "As the tortoise is so slow I can have a sleep!"
f The tortoise said, "Now he is asleep I can pass the hare."
g The hare shouted, "Oh no! The tortoise is at the winning post!"
h "I'm the winner!" the tortoise shouted happily.

Test 1 (pages 46 and 47)

1. a A girl is swimming.
   b Some boys are playing.
2. a sleep b torch
3. a dentist b clock
4. a In my bag I have a book, a pen, a ruler and a pencil.
   b March, April, May and June are months of the year.
5. a handle b eagle
6. a windmill b football
7. a winking b humming
8. a apple beetroot carrot date
   b sack skin slide snow
9. a head bread
   b round found
10. a **dis**agree b **un**lucky

Test 2 (pages 48 and 49)

1. a beautiful b tall

2 a wrist b knee

3 a help b rest

4 a you are b do not

5 a boxes b arches

6 a she b he

7 a neighs b hiss

8 a I got undressed and I went to bed.
b I tried to sleep but I could not.

9 a speak talk
b answer reply

10 a Jack said, "Have you seen my bag?"
b Sarah said, "It is by your chair."

Test 3 (pages 50 and 51)

1 a What is the weather like?
b Is it raining?

2 a cart b coach

3 a Wednesday b October

4 a Can you play tennis, Jack?
b Yes, I can.

5 a night b light

6 a toothbrush b handbag

7 a walked b slipped

8 a gorilla b plug

9 a fear near b dance chance

10 a replace b prehistoric

Test 4 (pages 52 and 53)

1 a fierce b slow

2 a gnome b thumb

3 a builder b footballer

4 a cannot b You are

5 a monkeys b babies

6 a yours b mine

7 a were b was

8 a The wind blew and the rain fell.
b I can hop but I can't skip.

9 a discover find
b shut close

10 a Anna said, "Do you want an apple?"
b Ben said, "May I have a banana instead?"